THE ODYSSEY

Homer

AGS®

American Guidance Service, Inc.
Circle Pines, Minnesota 55014-1796
1-800-328-2560

AGS ILLUSTRATED CLASSICS

Collection 1
Black Beauty, The Call of the Wild, Dr. Jekyll and Mr. Hyde, Dracula, Frankenstein, Huckleberry Finn, Moby Dick, The Red Badge of Courage, The Time Machine, Tom Sawyer, Treasure Island, 20,000 Leagues Under the Sea

Collection 2
The Great Adventures of Sherlock Holmes, Gulliver's Travels, The Hunchback of Notre Dame, The Invisible Man, Journey to the Center of the Earth, Kidnapped, The Mysterious Island, The Scarlet Letter, The Story of My Life, A Tale of Two Cities, The Three Musketeers, The War of the Worlds

Collection 3
Around the World in Eighty Days, Captains Courageous, A Connecticut Yankee in King Arthur's Court, The Hound of the Baskervilles, The House of the Seven Gables, Jany Eyre, The Last of the Mohicans, The Best of O. Henry, The Best of Poe, Two Years Before the Mast, White Fang, Wuthering Heights

Collection 4
Ben Hur, A Christmas Carol, The Food of the Gods, Ivanhoe, The Man in the Iron Mask, The Prince and the Pauper, The Prisoner of Zenda, The Return of the Native, Robinson Crusoe, The Scarlet Pimpernel, The Sea Wolf, The Swiss Family Robinson

Collection 5
Billy Budd, Crime and Punishment, Don Quixote, Great Expectations, Heidi, The Iliad, Lord Jim, The Mutiny on Board H.M.S. Bounty, The Odyssey, Oliver Twist, Pride and Prejudice, The Turn of the Screw

Shakespeare Collection
As You Like It, Hamlet, Julius Caesar, King Lear, Macbeth, The Merchant of Venice, A Midsummer Night's Dream, Othello, Romeo and Juliet, The Taming of the Shrew, The Tempest, Twelfth Night

© 1994 AGS® American Guidance Service, Inc., Circle Pines, Minnesota 55014-1796. All rights reserved, including translation. No part of this publication may be reproduced or transmitted in any form or by any means without written permission from the publisher.

Printed in the United States of America
ISBN 0-7854-0782-0
Product Number 40565
A 0 9 8 7 6 5 4 3 2

to the reader

Welcome to the AGS Illustrated Classics!

You are about to enter the world of great literature through pictures as well as words. Now you can actually see the great characters of literature as you read about them!

We want you to know that the costumes, hairstyles, room furnishings, and landscapes have all been carefully researched. No detail has been left out.

As you read, notice that important words are marked with an asterisk (*) and defined at the bottom of the page. Also watch for the scrolls that appear now and then. The scrolls contain important information that will add to your enjoyment of the story.

Now sit back and relax. We know that you will enjoy a great reading experience in the pages that follow.

—The Editors

about the author

Nearly thirty-two hundred years ago, long before the Greeks ever had a written language, Homer lived and told his stories. He was a bard—a wandering poet who kept his country's great legends alive by reciting them over and over.

Most people believe that Homer was blind. Perhaps he was able to compose and remember all his poems because he could see nothing to distract him from his thoughts. When he arrived at a village, or at the home of a wealthy man, all work stopped. A great feast was held, and everyone sat around afterward to listen to Homer's stories. The men and women, gods and goddesses he spoke about were part of Greece's legendary history. In their own way, his stories became one of the things that held this nation of city-states together.

Although Homer must have composed many poems during his lifetime, he is best known for the *Iliad,* his story of the Trojan War, and the *Odyssey,* the story of the wanderings of the hero Odysseus. Together, these two books are counted among the finest works ever composed by man.

The Odyssey
Homer

Adapted by
JOHN NORWOOD FAGO

Illustrated by
NESTOR REDONDO

a
VINCENT FAGO
production

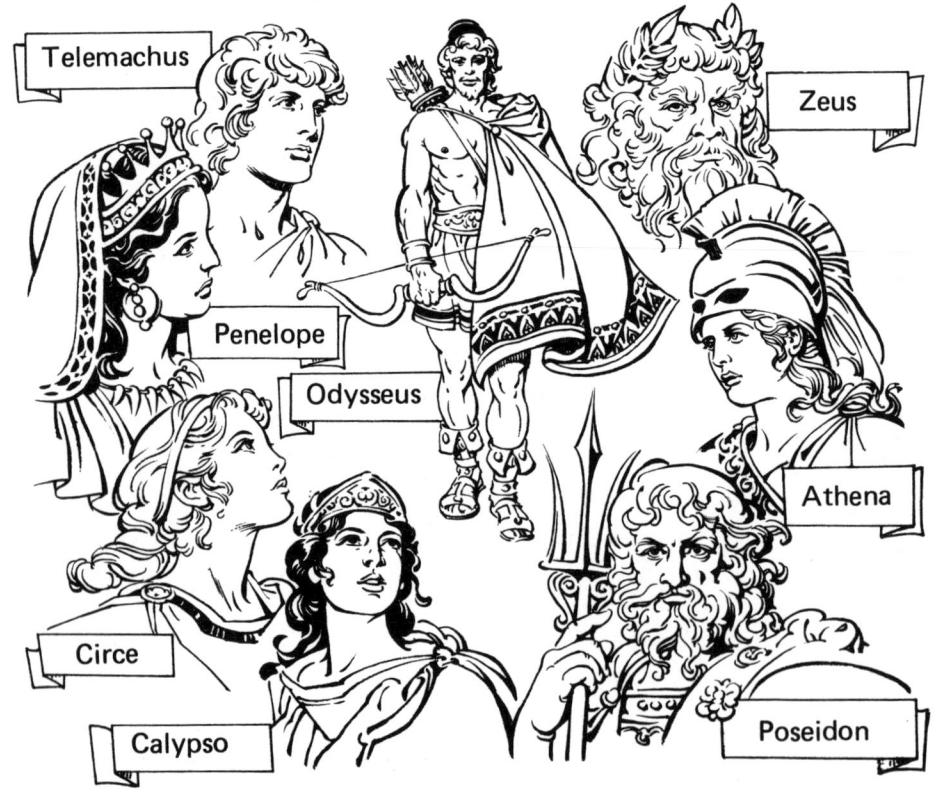

*something that is done to honor someone
**king of the gods and men of Greece

The Greeks believed in many gods. The most powerful of them all was Zeus, the god of the sky. But it was Zeus' brother, Poseidon, who caused Odysseus to have so much trouble when he came home from the war. Poseidon was the god of the sea.

When Odysseus was on his way home, a great storm sank his ship. The last of his men were drowned. The sea carried Odysseus to the island of Ogygia, where a goddess* named Calypso lived. Here Odysseus stayed for nearly ten years, unable to return home.

Poor Odysseus! For so long you have been sad. But why do you sit alone on the shore? Your ships and your men are gone forever.

Come, Odysseus. You must forget your wife and son. I will let you live forever if you will stay with me.

You are lovely, Calypso, but how can I forget the people who have not forgotten *me*?

*female god

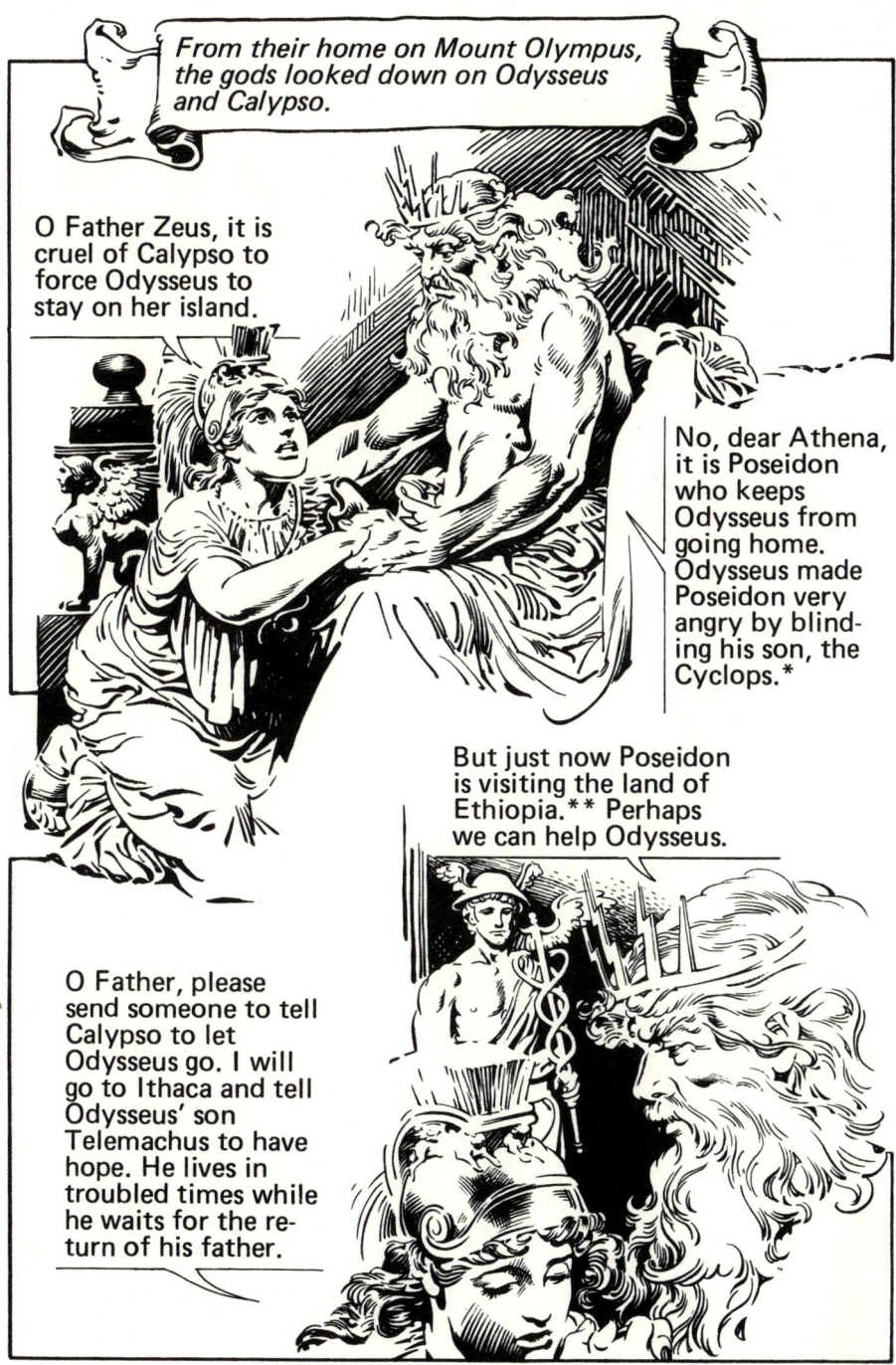

*a one-eyed giant
**part of Africa

*someone that sings and plays a musical instrument

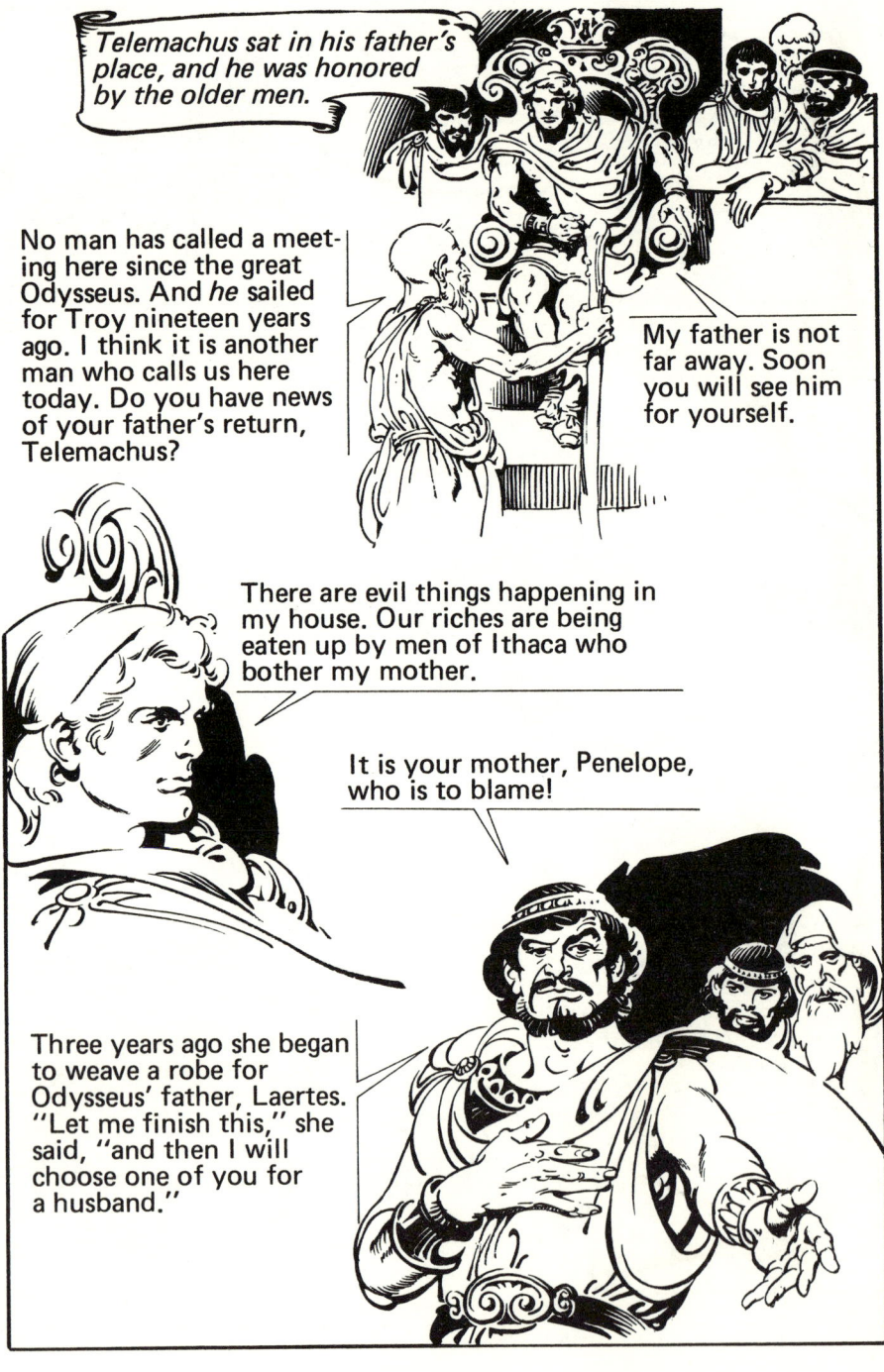

*people who lived on the island of Scheria in the Aegean Sea

*something that can't be seen

*a plant

The Odyssey 37

When we drew near to where the Sirens lived, I knew that I should be the only one to hear their song.

My sailors, I will plug your ears with beeswax. Then you will tie me to the mast.* No matter what I do, you must keep rowing until we have gone past the rocks.

ODYSSEUS... COME TO US... COME

Let me go! Let me go!

But my men heard nothing, and we passed safely by the rocks.

Thank you, men. It was the most beautiful sound that my ears have ever heard.

*one of the tall poles to which a ship's sails are fastened

*someone who takes care of sheep

*someone who cares for a herd of pigs

*important person

*to shoot a bow and arrow at a target

*a yellow material that smells bad but was often used for cleaning

words to know

prophet	tempted	minstrel
swineherd	herb	doom
archery	goddess	Hermes

questions

1. How did Odysseus happen to land on the island of Ogygia—alone—after the Trojan War ended? How long did he stay on Ogygia?
2. Of the following gods and goddesses, which ones were friendly to Odysseus and which ones worked against him: Zeus, Athena, Poseidon, Hermes, Aeolus, the Sirens?
3. Why did Penelope and Telemachus have such a hard time in Ithaca while Odysseus was away?
4. How did Odysseus and his men escape from the cave of the Cyclops?
5. How did the dead prophet Tiresias help Odysseus? Did his prophecy come true?
6. When Odysseus reached Ithaca at last, why did he stay with the swineherd Eumaeus instead of going directly home?
7. Although there are only hints in the story, can you tell why it was a custom at that time to honor and help all travelers and beggars?
8. How did Penelope prove to herself who Odysseus really was?